My Political Memories, Dreams And Nightmares

My Personal Political Tracker

EZLifeTrackers.com

Created: By Steve Mitchell

We all have stresses in our life. We also have things that make us happy and get us excited. In America, politics is probably one of those things that stresses us and also makes us happy and excited at different times.

Start to record your political thoughts, feelings, dreams and even nightmares as reminders of what you thought and felt and perhaps as a way to reduce your stress. By writing down what you are thinking and feeling as you watch and or participate in our political process can be cathartic. Just watching and listening to what is going on makes you a willing or unwilling participant. Local or national politics impacts all of us.

DO YOU HAVE A GREAT MEMORY? Most of us need reminders...

We have made EZ Life Trackers for some of the many popular places throughout the world and for many of the activities in life, like participating in politics.

My Political Memories, Dreams And Nightmares, My Personal Political Tracker is 8.5" x 11", with a total of 100 pages, 98 for data entry. The book enables you to record your thoughts, feelings, dreams and even nightmares as you participate or listen to what is going on in politics every day. Anger, hate, pride, hope, enthusiasm, patriotism or whatever you are feeling just write it down. Record the dates as well.

Writing things down can help you recognize and process your emotions. By forcing yourself to put your emotions to writing, you can process your thoughts (whether positive or negative) and feelings at a much deeper level than simply thinking about it. By writing things down you may also find that you feel more relaxed since you have had the opportunity to express what you were thinking and feeling rather than just keeping it inside.

Extend your memories by regularly updating My Political Memories, Dreams and Nightmares, My Personal Political Tracker.

Hopefully you can survive the political events that surround us every day and I hope that this EZ Life Tracker proves to be an invaluable record of your political thoughts, feelings, dreams and nightmares during the years.

Record Your Political Thoughts, Feelings, Dreams and Nightmares. Just went to a rally or watched the news? Include anger, hate, pride, hope, enthusiasm patriotism or whatever you are feeling just write it down. Also include the dates.

Record Your Political Thoughts, Feelings, Dreams and Nightmares. Just went to a rally or watched the news? Include anger, hate, pride, hope, enthusiasm patriotism or whatever you are feeling just write it down. Also include the dates.

Record Your Political Thoughts, Feelings, Dreams and Nightmares. Just went to a rally or watched the news? Include anger, hate, pride, hope, enthusiasm patriotism or whatever you are feeling just write it down. Also include the dates.

Record Your Political Thoughts, Feelings, Dreams and Nightmares. Just went to a rally or watched the news? Include anger, hate, pride, hope, enthusiasm patriotism or whatever you are feeling just write it down. Also include the dates.

Record Your Political Thoughts, Feelings, Dreams and Nightmares. Just went to a rally or watched the news? Include anger, hate, pride, hope, enthusiasm patriotism or whatever you are feeling just write it down. Also include the dates.

Record Your Political Thoughts, Feelings, Dreams and Nightmares. Just went to a rally or watched the news? Include anger, hate, pride, hope, enthusiasm patriotism or whatever you are feeling just write it down. Also include the dates.

____
____
____
____
____
____
____
____
____
____
____
____
____
____
____
____
____
____
____
____
____
____
____
____

Record Your Political Thoughts, Feelings, Dreams and Nightmares. Just went to a rally or watched the news? Include anger, hate, pride, hope, enthusiasm patriotism or whatever you are feeling just write it down. Also include the dates.

Record Your Political Thoughts, Feelings, Dreams and Nightmares. Just went to a rally or watched the news? Include anger, hate, pride, hope, enthusiasm patriotism or whatever you are feeling just write it down. Also include the dates.

Record Your Political Thoughts, Feelings, Dreams and Nightmares. Just went to a rally or watched the news? Include anger, hate, pride, hope, enthusiasm patriotism or whatever you are feeling just write it down. Also include the dates.

Record Your Political Thoughts, Feelings, Dreams and Nightmares. Just went to a rally or watched the news? Include anger, hate, pride, hope, enthusiasm patriotism or whatever you are feeling just write it down. Also include the dates.

Record Your Political Thoughts, Feelings, Dreams and Nightmares. Just went to a rally or watched the news? Include anger, hate, pride, hope, enthusiasm patriotism or whatever you are feeling just write it down. Also include the dates.

____

____

____

____

____

____

____

____

____

____

____

____

____

____

____

____

____

____

____

____

____

____

____

____

____

Record Your Political Thoughts, Feelings, Dreams and Nightmares. Just went to a rally or watched the news? Include anger, hate, pride, hope, enthusiasm patriotism or whatever you are feeling just write it down. Also include the dates.

Record Your Political Thoughts, Feelings, Dreams and Nightmares. Just went to a rally or watched the news? Include anger, hate, pride, hope, enthusiasm patriotism or whatever you are feeling just write it down. Also include the dates.

Record Your Political Thoughts, Feelings, Dreams and Nightmares. Just went to a rally or watched the news? Include anger, hate, pride, hope, enthusiasm patriotism or whatever you are feeling just write it down. Also include the dates.

Record Your Political Thoughts, Feelings, Dreams and Nightmares. Just went to a rally or watched the news? Include anger, hate, pride, hope, enthusiasm patriotism or whatever you are feeling just write it down. Also include the dates.

Record Your Political Thoughts, Feelings, Dreams and Nightmares. Just went to a rally or watched the news? Include anger, hate, pride, hope, enthusiasm patriotism or whatever you are feeling just write it down. Also include the dates.

Record Your Political Thoughts, Feelings, Dreams and Nightmares. Just went to a rally or watched the news? Include anger, hate, pride, hope, enthusiasm patriotism or whatever you are feeling just write it down. Also include the dates.

Record Your Political Thoughts, Feelings, Dreams and Nightmares. Just went to a rally or watched the news? Include anger, hate, pride, hope, enthusiasm patriotism or whatever you are feeling just write it down. Also include the dates.

Record Your Political Thoughts, Feelings, Dreams and Nightmares. Just went to a rally or watched the news? Include anger, hate, pride, hope, enthusiasm patriotism or whatever you are feeling just write it down. Also include the dates.

Record Your Political Thoughts, Feelings, Dreams and Nightmares. Just went to a rally or watched the news? Include anger, hate, pride, hope, enthusiasm patriotism or whatever you are feeling just write it down. Also include the dates.

____

____

____

____

____

____

____

____

____

____

____

____

____

____

____

____

____

____

____

____

____

____

____

____

Record Your Political Thoughts, Feelings, Dreams and Nightmares. Just went to a rally or watched the news? Include anger, hate, pride, hope, enthusiasm patriotism or whatever you are feeling just write it down. Also include the dates.

Record Your Political Thoughts, Feelings, Dreams and Nightmares. Just went to a rally or watched the news? Include anger, hate, pride, hope, enthusiasm patriotism or whatever you are feeling just write it down. Also include the dates.

Record Your Political Thoughts, Feelings, Dreams and Nightmares. Just went to a rally or watched the news? Include anger, hate, pride, hope, enthusiasm patriotism or whatever you are feeling just write it down. Also include the dates.

Record Your Political Thoughts, Feelings, Dreams and Nightmares. Just went to a rally or watched the news? Include anger, hate, pride, hope, enthusiasm patriotism or whatever you are feeling just write it down. Also include the dates.

Record Your Political Thoughts, Feelings, Dreams and Nightmares. Just went to a rally or watched the news? Include anger, hate, pride, hope, enthusiasm patriotism or whatever you are feeling just write it down. Also include the dates.

Record Your Political Thoughts, Feelings, Dreams and Nightmares. Just went to a rally or watched the news? Include anger, hate, pride, hope, enthusiasm patriotism or whatever you are feeling just write it down. Also include the dates.

Record Your Political Thoughts, Feelings, Dreams and Nightmares. Just went to a rally or watched the news? Include anger, hate, pride, hope, enthusiasm patriotism or whatever you are feeling just write it down. Also include the dates.

Record Your Political Thoughts, Feelings, Dreams and Nightmares. Just went to a rally or watched the news? Include anger, hate, pride, hope, enthusiasm patriotism or whatever you are feeling just write it down. Also include the dates.

Record Your Political Thoughts, Feelings, Dreams and Nightmares. Just went to a rally or watched the news? Include anger, hate, pride, hope, enthusiasm patriotism or whatever you are feeling just write it down. Also include the dates.

Record Your Political Thoughts, Feelings, Dreams and Nightmares. Just went to a rally or watched the news? Include anger, hate, pride, hope, enthusiasm patriotism or whatever you are feeling just write it down. Also include the dates.

Record Your Political Thoughts, Feelings, Dreams and Nightmares. Just went to a rally or watched the news? Include anger, hate, pride, hope, enthusiasm patriotism or whatever you are feeling just write it down. Also include the dates.

Record Your Political Thoughts, Feelings, Dreams and Nightmares. Just went to a rally or watched the news? Include anger, hate, pride, hope, enthusiasm patriotism or whatever you are feeling just write it down. Also include the dates.

Record Your Political Thoughts, Feelings, Dreams and Nightmares. Just went to a rally or watched the news? Include anger, hate, pride, hope, enthusiasm patriotism or whatever you are feeling just write it down. Also include the dates.

Record Your Political Thoughts, Feelings, Dreams and Nightmares. Just went to a rally or watched the news? Include anger, hate, pride, hope, enthusiasm patriotism or whatever you are feeling just write it down. Also include the dates.

Record Your Political Thoughts, Feelings, Dreams and Nightmares. Just went to a rally or watched the news? Include anger, hate, pride, hope, enthusiasm patriotism or whatever you are feeling just write it down. Also include the dates.

Record Your Political Thoughts, Feelings, Dreams and Nightmares. Just went to a rally or watched the news? Include anger, hate, pride, hope, enthusiasm patriotism or whatever you are feeling just write it down. Also include the dates.

Record Your Political Thoughts, Feelings, Dreams and Nightmares. Just went to a rally or watched the news? Include anger, hate, pride, hope, enthusiasm patriotism or whatever you are feeling just write it down. Also include the dates.

Record Your Political Thoughts, Feelings, Dreams and Nightmares. Just went to a rally or watched the news? Include anger, hate, pride, hope, enthusiasm patriotism or whatever you are feeling just write it down. Also include the dates.

Record Your Political Thoughts, Feelings, Dreams and Nightmares. Just went to a rally or watched the news? Include anger, hate, pride, hope, enthusiasm patriotism or whatever you are feeling just write it down. Also include the dates.

Record Your Political Thoughts, Feelings, Dreams and Nightmares. Just went to a rally or watched the news? Include anger, hate, pride, hope, enthusiasm patriotism or whatever you are feeling just write it down. Also include the dates.

Record Your Political Thoughts, Feelings, Dreams and Nightmares. Just went to a rally or watched the news? Include anger, hate, pride, hope, enthusiasm patriotism or whatever you are feeling just write it down. Also include the dates.

Record Your Political Thoughts, Feelings, Dreams and Nightmares. Just went to a rally or watched the news? Include anger, hate, pride, hope, enthusiasm patriotism or whatever you are feeling just write it down. Also include the dates.

Record Your Political Thoughts, Feelings, Dreams and Nightmares. Just went to a rally or watched the news? Include anger, hate, pride, hope, enthusiasm patriotism or whatever you are feeling just write it down. Also include the dates.

Record Your Political Thoughts, Feelings, Dreams and Nightmares. Just went to a rally or watched the news? Include anger, hate, pride, hope, enthusiasm patriotism or whatever you are feeling just write it down. Also include the dates.

Record Your Political Thoughts, Feelings, Dreams and Nightmares. Just went to a rally or watched the news? Include anger, hate, pride, hope, enthusiasm patriotism or whatever you are feeling just write it down. Also include the dates.

____
____
____
____
____
____
____
____
____
____
____
____
____
____
____
____
____
____
____
____
____
____
____
____
____

Record Your Political Thoughts, Feelings, Dreams and Nightmares. Just went to a rally or watched the news? Include anger, hate, pride, hope, enthusiasm patriotism or whatever you are feeling just write it down. Also include the dates.

Record Your Political Thoughts, Feelings, Dreams and Nightmares. Just went to a rally or watched the news? Include anger, hate, pride, hope, enthusiasm patriotism or whatever you are feeling just write it down. Also include the dates.

Record Your Political Thoughts, Feelings, Dreams and Nightmares. Just went to a rally or watched the news? Include anger, hate, pride, hope, enthusiasm patriotism or whatever you are feeling just write it down. Also include the dates.

Record Your Political Thoughts, Feelings, Dreams and Nightmares. Just went to a rally or watched the news? Include anger, hate, pride, hope, enthusiasm patriotism or whatever you are feeling just write it down. Also include the dates.

Record Your Political Thoughts, Feelings, Dreams and Nightmares. Just went to a rally or watched the news? Include anger, hate, pride, hope, enthusiasm patriotism or whatever you are feeling just write it down. Also include the dates.

Record Your Political Thoughts, Feelings, Dreams and Nightmares. Just went to a rally or watched the news? Include anger, hate, pride, hope, enthusiasm patriotism or whatever you are feeling just write it down. Also include the dates.

Record Your Political Thoughts, Feelings, Dreams and Nightmares. Just went to a rally or watched the news? Include anger, hate, pride, hope, enthusiasm patriotism or whatever you are feeling just write it down. Also include the dates.

Record Your Political Thoughts, Feelings, Dreams and Nightmares. Just went to a rally or watched the news? Include anger, hate, pride, hope, enthusiasm patriotism or whatever you are feeling just write it down. Also include the dates.

Record Your Political Thoughts, Feelings, Dreams and Nightmares. Just went to a rally or watched the news? Include anger, hate, pride, hope, enthusiasm patriotism or whatever you are feeling just write it down. Also include the dates.

Record Your Political Thoughts, Feelings, Dreams and Nightmares. Just went to a rally or watched the news? Include anger, hate, pride, hope, enthusiasm patriotism or whatever you are feeling just write it down. Also include the dates.

Record Your Political Thoughts, Feelings, Dreams and Nightmares. Just went to a rally or watched the news? Include anger, hate, pride, hope, enthusiasm patriotism or whatever you are feeling just write it down. Also include the dates.

Record Your Political Thoughts, Feelings, Dreams and Nightmares. Just went to a rally or watched the news? Include anger, hate, pride, hope, enthusiasm patriotism or whatever you are feeling just write it down. Also include the dates.

Record Your Political Thoughts, Feelings, Dreams and Nightmares. Just went to a rally or watched the news? Include anger, hate, pride, hope, enthusiasm patriotism or whatever you are feeling just write it down. Also include the dates.

____
____
____
____
____
____
____
____
____
____
____
____
____
____
____
____
____
____
____
____
____
____
____
____
____

Record Your Political Thoughts, Feelings, Dreams and Nightmares. Just went to a rally or watched the news? Include anger, hate, pride, hope, enthusiasm patriotism or whatever you are feeling just write it down. Also include the dates.

Record Your Political Thoughts, Feelings, Dreams and Nightmares. Just went to a rally or watched the news? Include anger, hate, pride, hope, enthusiasm patriotism or whatever you are feeling just write it down. Also include the dates.

Record Your Political Thoughts, Feelings, Dreams and Nightmares. Just went to a rally or watched the news? Include anger, hate, pride, hope, enthusiasm patriotism or whatever you are feeling just write it down. Also include the dates.

Record Your Political Thoughts, Feelings, Dreams and Nightmares. Just went to a rally or watched the news? Include anger, hate, pride, hope, enthusiasm patriotism or whatever you are feeling just write it down. Also include the dates.

Record Your Political Thoughts, Feelings, Dreams and Nightmares. Just went to a rally or watched the news? Include anger, hate, pride, hope, enthusiasm patriotism or whatever you are feeling just write it down. Also include the dates.

Record Your Political Thoughts, Feelings, Dreams and Nightmares. Just went to a rally or watched the news? Include anger, hate, pride, hope, enthusiasm patriotism or whatever you are feeling just write it down. Also include the dates.

Record Your Political Thoughts, Feelings, Dreams and Nightmares. Just went to a rally or watched the news? Include anger, hate, pride, hope, enthusiasm patriotism or whatever you are feeling just write it down. Also include the dates.

Record Your Political Thoughts, Feelings, Dreams and Nightmares. Just went to a rally or watched the news? Include anger, hate, pride, hope, enthusiasm patriotism or whatever you are feeling just write it down. Also include the dates.

Record Your Political Thoughts, Feelings, Dreams and Nightmares. Just went to a rally or watched the news? Include anger, hate, pride, hope, enthusiasm patriotism or whatever you are feeling just write it down. Also include the dates.

Record Your Political Thoughts, Feelings, Dreams and Nightmares. Just went to a rally or watched the news? Include anger, hate, pride, hope, enthusiasm patriotism or whatever you are feeling just write it down. Also include the dates.

Record Your Political Thoughts, Feelings, Dreams and Nightmares. Just went to a rally or watched the news? Include anger, hate, pride, hope, enthusiasm patriotism or whatever you are feeling just write it down. Also include the dates.

Record Your Political Thoughts, Feelings, Dreams and Nightmares. Just went to a rally or watched the news? Include anger, hate, pride, hope, enthusiasm patriotism or whatever you are feeling just write it down. Also include the dates.

Record Your Political Thoughts, Feelings, Dreams and Nightmares. Just went to a rally or watched the news? Include anger, hate, pride, hope, enthusiasm patriotism or whatever you are feeling just write it down. Also include the dates.

Record Your Political Thoughts, Feelings, Dreams and Nightmares. Just went to a rally or watched the news? Include anger, hate, pride, hope, enthusiasm patriotism or whatever you are feeling just write it down. Also include the dates.

Record Your Political Thoughts, Feelings, Dreams and Nightmares. Just went to a rally or watched the news? Include anger, hate, pride, hope, enthusiasm patriotism or whatever you are feeling just write it down. Also include the dates.

Record Your Political Thoughts, Feelings, Dreams and Nightmares. Just went to a rally or watched the news? Include anger, hate, pride, hope, enthusiasm patriotism or whatever you are feeling just write it down. Also include the dates.

Record Your Political Thoughts, Feelings, Dreams and Nightmares. Just went to a rally or watched the news? Include anger, hate, pride, hope, enthusiasm patriotism or whatever you are feeling just write it down. Also include the dates.

Record Your Political Thoughts, Feelings, Dreams and Nightmares. Just went to a rally or watched the news? Include anger, hate, pride, hope, enthusiasm patriotism or whatever you are feeling just write it down. Also include the dates.

Record Your Political Thoughts, Feelings, Dreams and Nightmares. Just went to a rally or watched the news? Include anger, hate, pride, hope, enthusiasm patriotism or whatever you are feeling just write it down. Also include the dates.

Record Your Political Thoughts, Feelings, Dreams and Nightmares. Just went to a rally or watched the news? Include anger, hate, pride, hope, enthusiasm patriotism or whatever you are feeling just write it down. Also include the dates.

Record Your Political Thoughts, Feelings, Dreams and Nightmares. Just went to a rally or watched the news? Include anger, hate, pride, hope, enthusiasm patriotism or whatever you are feeling just write it down. Also include the dates.

____

____

____

____

____

____

____

____

____

____

____

____

____

____

____

____

____

____

____

____

____

____

____

____

____

____

Record Your Political Thoughts, Feelings, Dreams and Nightmares. Just went to a rally or watched the news? Include anger, hate, pride, hope, enthusiasm patriotism or whatever you are feeling just write it down. Also include the dates.

Record Your Political Thoughts, Feelings, Dreams and Nightmares. Just went to a rally or watched the news? Include anger, hate, pride, hope, enthusiasm patriotism or whatever you are feeling just write it down. Also include the dates.

Record Your Political Thoughts, Feelings, Dreams and Nightmares. Just went to a rally or watched the news? Include anger, hate, pride, hope, enthusiasm patriotism or whatever you are feeling just write it down. Also include the dates.

Record Your Political Thoughts, Feelings, Dreams and Nightmares. Just went to a rally or watched the news? Include anger, hate, pride, hope, enthusiasm patriotism or whatever you are feeling just write it down. Also include the dates.

Record Your Political Thoughts, Feelings, Dreams and Nightmares. Just went to a rally or watched the news? Include anger, hate, pride, hope, enthusiasm patriotism or whatever you are feeling just write it down. Also include the dates.

Record Your Political Thoughts, Feelings, Dreams and Nightmares. Just went to a rally or watched the news? Include anger, hate, pride, hope, enthusiasm patriotism or whatever you are feeling just write it down. Also include the dates.

Record Your Political Thoughts, Feelings, Dreams and Nightmares. Just went to a rally or watched the news? Include anger, hate, pride, hope, enthusiasm patriotism or whatever you are feeling just write it down. Also include the dates.

Record Your Political Thoughts, Feelings, Dreams and Nightmares. Just went to a rally or watched the news? Include anger, hate, pride, hope, enthusiasm patriotism or whatever you are feeling just write it down. Also include the dates.

Record Your Political Thoughts, Feelings, Dreams and Nightmares. Just went to a rally or watched the news? Include anger, hate, pride, hope, enthusiasm patriotism or whatever you are feeling just write it down. Also include the dates.

Record Your Political Thoughts, Feelings, Dreams and Nightmares. Just went to a rally or watched the news? Include anger, hate, pride, hope, enthusiasm patriotism or whatever you are feeling just write it down. Also include the dates.

Record Your Political Thoughts, Feelings, Dreams and Nightmares. Just went to a rally or watched the news? Include anger, hate, pride, hope, enthusiasm patriotism or whatever you are feeling just write it down. Also include the dates.

Record Your Political Thoughts, Feelings, Dreams and Nightmares. Just went to a rally or watched the news? Include anger, hate, pride, hope, enthusiasm patriotism or whatever you are feeling just write it down. Also include the dates.

Record Your Political Thoughts, Feelings, Dreams and Nightmares. Just went to a rally or watched the news? Include anger, hate, pride, hope, enthusiasm patriotism or whatever you are feeling just write it down. Also include the dates.

Record Your Political Thoughts, Feelings, Dreams and Nightmares. Just went to a rally or watched the news? Include anger, hate, pride, hope, enthusiasm patriotism or whatever you are feeling just write it down. Also include the dates.

Record Your Political Thoughts, Feelings, Dreams and Nightmares. Just went to a rally or watched the news? Include anger, hate, pride, hope, enthusiasm patriotism or whatever you are feeling just write it down. Also include the dates.

Record Your Political Thoughts, Feelings, Dreams and Nightmares. Just went to a rally or watched the news? Include anger, hate, pride, hope, enthusiasm patriotism or whatever you are feeling just write it down. Also include the dates.

Record Your Political Thoughts, Feelings, Dreams and Nightmares. Just went to a rally or watched the news? Include anger, hate, pride, hope, enthusiasm patriotism or whatever you are feeling just write it down. Also include the dates.

Record Your Political Thoughts, Feelings, Dreams and Nightmares. Just went to a rally or watched the news? Include anger, hate, pride, hope, enthusiasm patriotism or whatever you are feeling just write it down. Also include the dates.

Record Your Political Thoughts, Feelings, Dreams and Nightmares. Just went to a rally or watched the news? Include anger, hate, pride, hope, enthusiasm patriotism or whatever you are feeling just write it down. Also include the dates.